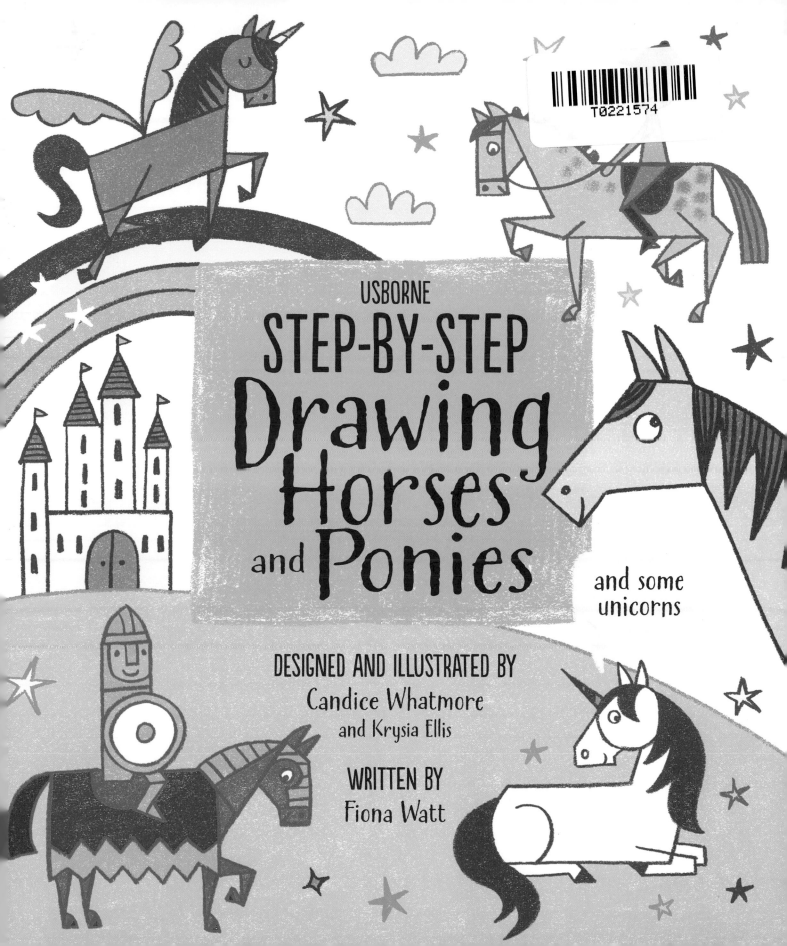

USBORNE
STEP-BY-STEP
Drawing
Horses
and Ponies

and some
unicorns

DESIGNED AND ILLUSTRATED BY
Candice Whatmore
and Krysia Ellis

WRITTEN BY
Fiona Watt

How to draw a horse's head

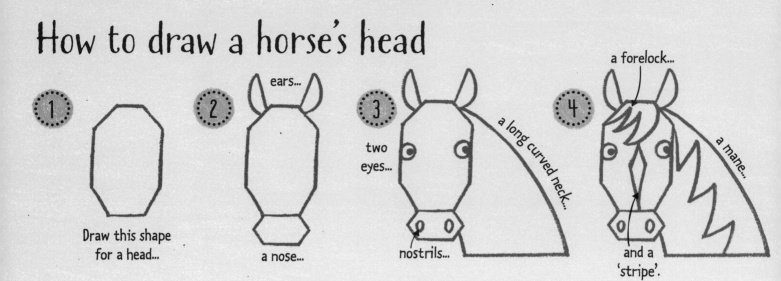

1 Draw this shape for a head...

2 ears... a nose...

3 two eyes... a long curved neck... nostrils...

4 a forelock... a mane... and a 'stripe'.

Your turn...

Try this...

Horses can be identified by markings on their heads. Here are some of them that you could add to your drawings.

Star   Snip   Stripe   Blaze

How to draw a head side-on

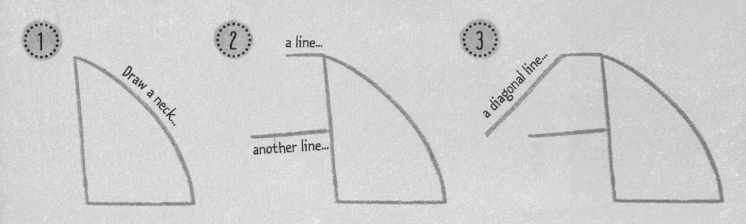

1 Draw a neck...

2 a line...
another line...

3 a diagonal line...

Your turn...

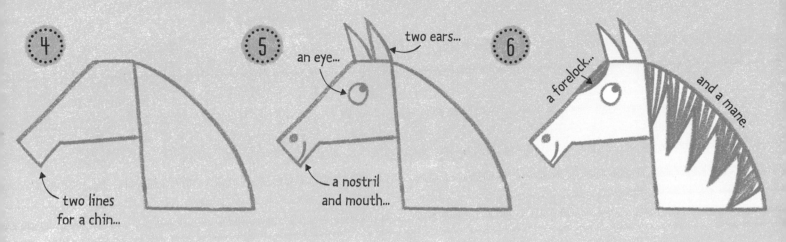

④ two lines for a chin...

⑤ an eye... two ears... a nostril and mouth...

⑥ a forelock... and a mane.

How to draw a whole horse

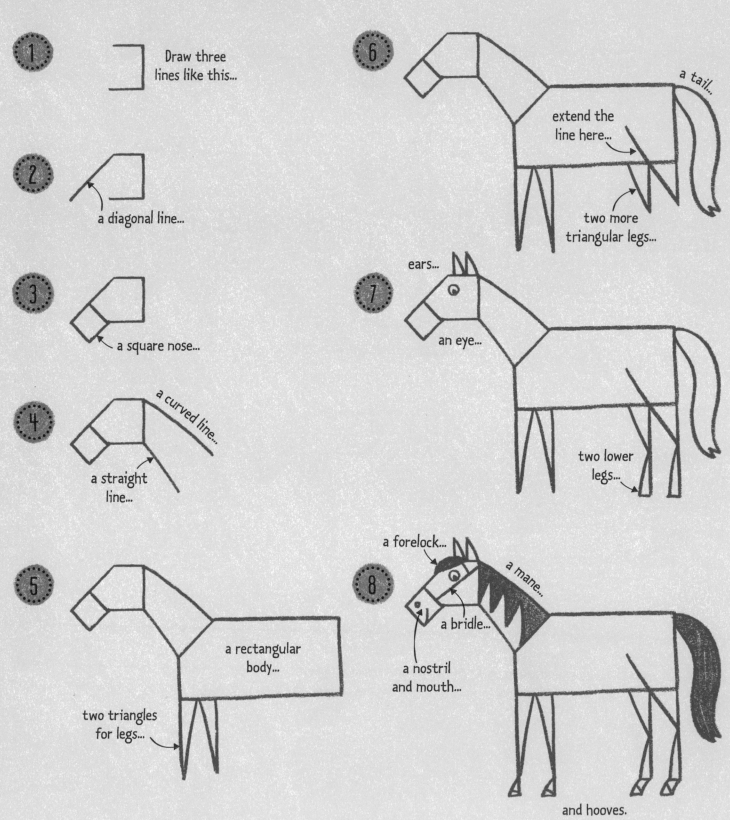

1 Draw three lines like this...

2 a diagonal line...

3 a square nose...

4 a curved line...
a straight line...

5 a rectangular body...
two triangles for legs...

6 extend the line here...
a tail...
two more triangular legs...

7 ears...
an eye...
two lower legs...

8 a forelock...
a mane...
a bridle...
a nostril and mouth...
and hooves.

Your turn...

Filling in your horses

Horses' coats come in lots of different colours, markings and patterns. Here are some of the most common types of coats. You could use the ideas to fill in your drawings, or to create combinations of your own.

Liver chestnut

Your turn...

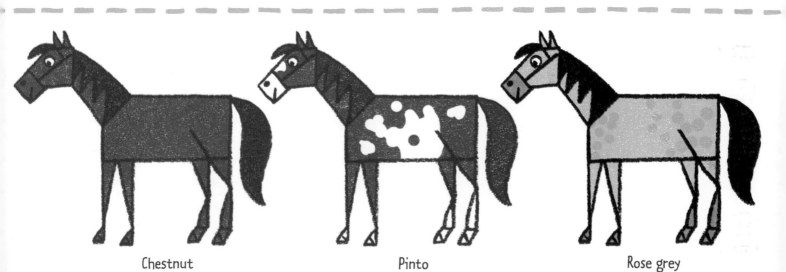

Chestnut

Pinto

Rose grey

White   Amber   Black

Blue roan   Palomino   Appaloosa

How to draw a unicorn's head

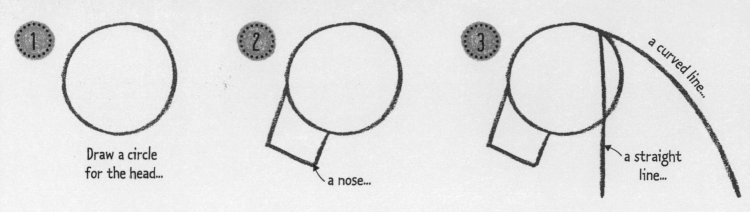

1 Draw a circle for the head...

2 a nose...

3 a curved line...
a straight line...

Your turn...

4

a forelock...

an eye...

a mane...

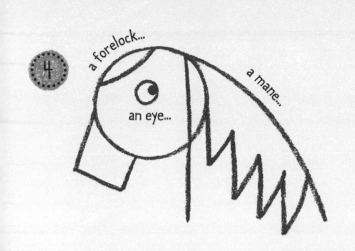

5

a horn...

and two ears.

Then, fill in the mane and forelock.

a nostril and a mouth...

How to draw a whole unicorn

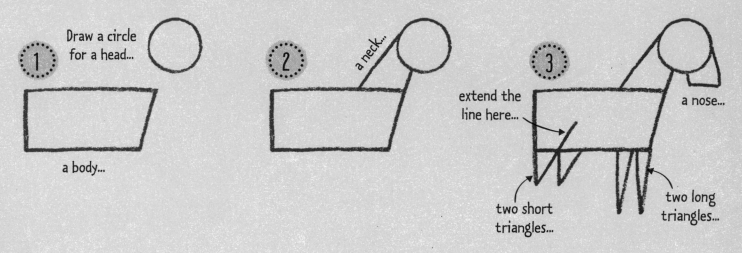

1 Draw a circle for a head...

a body...

2 a neck...

3 extend the line here...

a nose...

two short triangles...

two long triangles...

Your turn...

4 two ears... a horn...

two small triangles...

5 a forelock and a mane...

a tail...

6 lines for hair... an eye...

a nose and mouth...

and four hooves.

You could add some clouds and stars to make your drawing more magical.

How to draw a flying unicorn

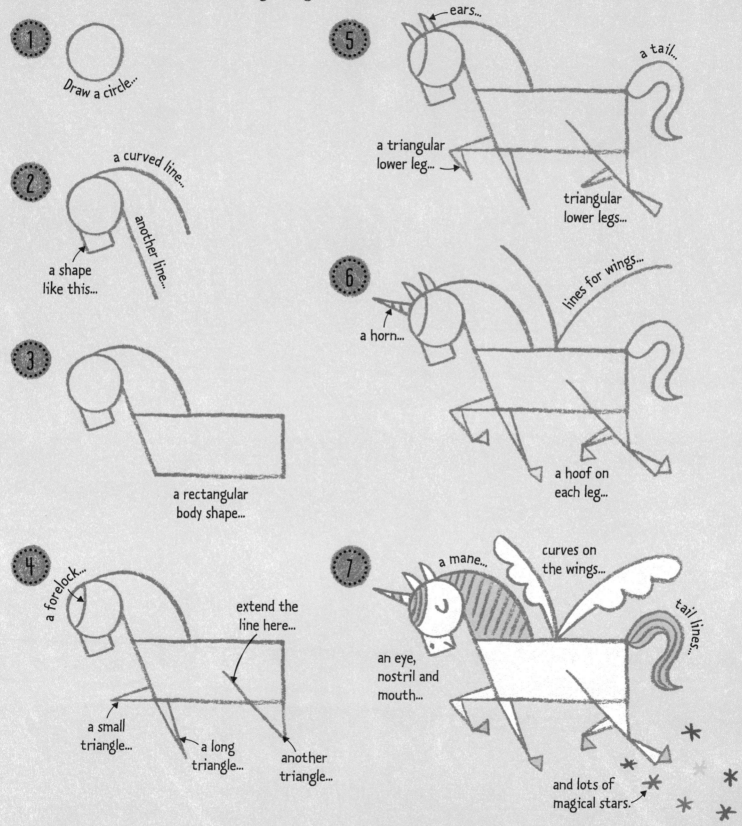

1 Draw a circle...

2 a curved line... a shape like this... another line...

3 a rectangular body shape...

4 a forelock... extend the line here... a small triangle... a long triangle... another triangle...

5 ears... a tail... a triangular lower leg... triangular lower legs...

6 a horn... lines for wings... a hoof on each leg...

7 a mane... curves on the wings... tail lines... an eye, nostril and mouth... and lots of magical stars.

Your turn...

How to draw a horse eating

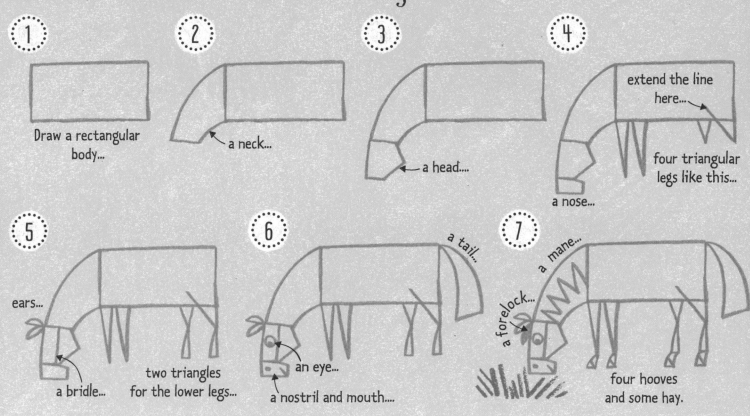

① Draw a rectangular body...

② a neck...

③ a head....

④ extend the line here... a nose... four triangular legs like this...

⑤ ears... a bridle... two triangles for the lower legs...

⑥ a tail... an eye... a nostril and mouth.....

⑦ a mane... a forelock... four hooves and some hay.

Your turn...

How to draw a pony

Your turn...

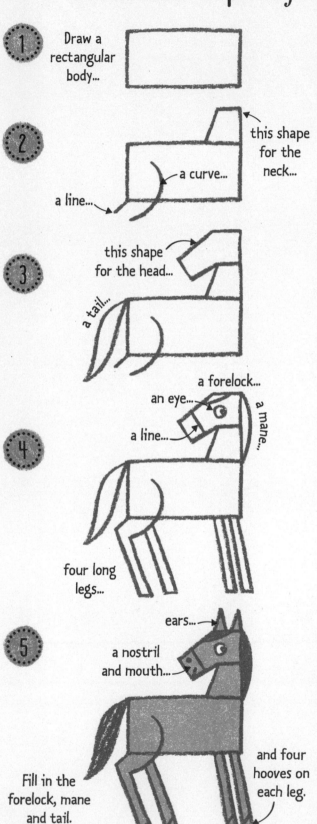

1 Draw a rectangular body...

2 this shape for the neck...
a curve...
a line...

3 this shape for the head...
a tail...

4 a forelock...
an eye...
a line...
a mane...
four long legs...

5 ears...
a nostril and mouth...
and four hooves on each leg.
Fill in the forelock, mane and tail.

18

How to draw a saddle

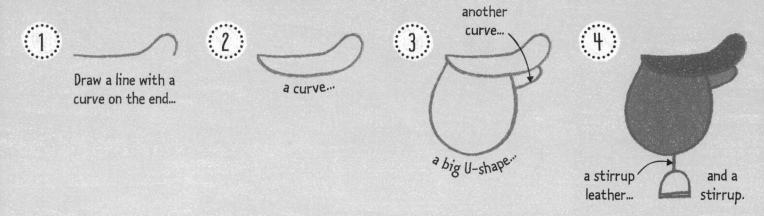

1 Draw a line with a curve on the end...

2 a curve...

3 a big U-shape... another curve...

4 a stirrup leather... and a stirrup.

Your turn...

How to draw a galloping horse

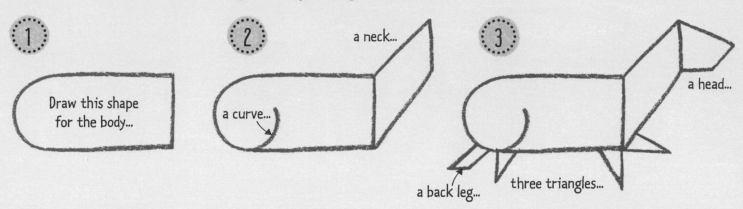

1

Draw this shape for the body...

2

a curve...

a neck...

3

a head...

a back leg...

three triangles...

Your turn...

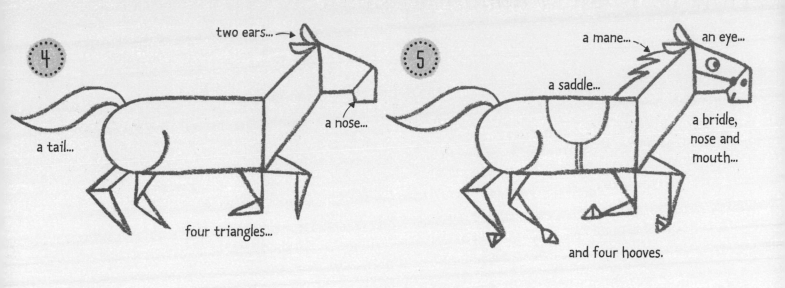

4

two ears... →

a tail...

a nose...

four triangles...

5

a mane... →

a saddle...

an eye...

a bridle,
nose and
mouth...

and four hooves.

How to draw a rider on a galloping horse

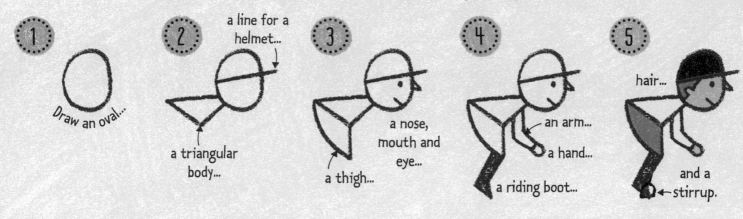

1 Draw an oval...

2 a line for a helmet... a triangular body...

3 a nose, mouth and eye... a thigh...

4 an arm... a hand... a riding boot...

5 hair... and a stirrup.

Your turn...

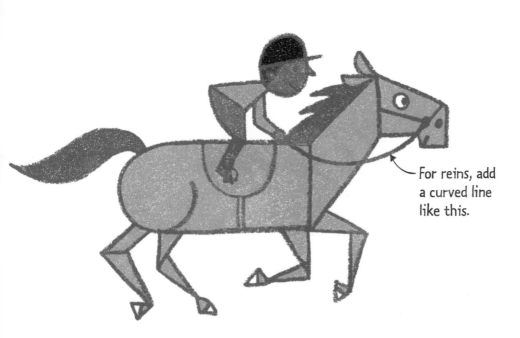

For reins, add a curved line like this.

Try this...

Draw some riders on these galloping horses.

How to draw a rosette

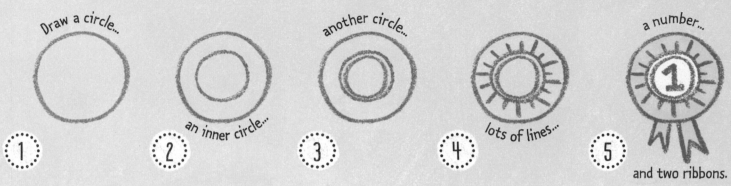

Draw a circle...

1

an inner circle...

2

another circle...

3

lots of lines...

4

a number...

5

and two ribbons.

Try this...

Add some rosettes around the necks of these show ponies.

Your turn...

...and a trophy.

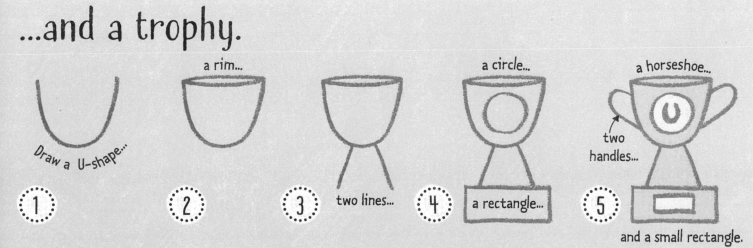

a rim...

a circle...

a horseshoe...

Draw a U-shape...

two lines...

a rectangle...

two handles...

and a small rectangle.

① ② ③ ④ ⑤

How to draw a sleeping horse

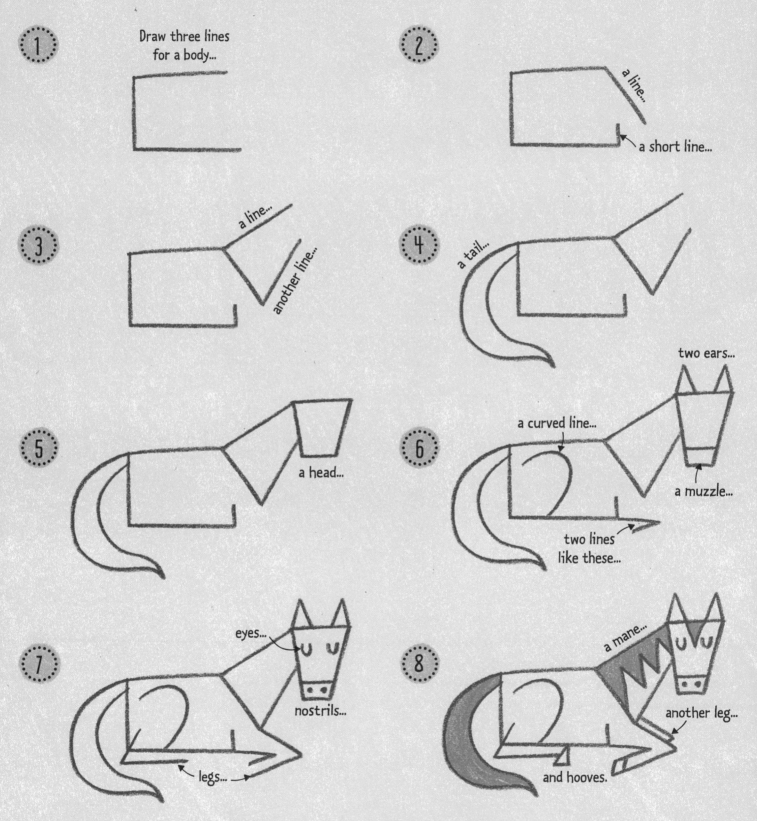

1. Draw three lines for a body...

2. a line... a short line...

3. a line... another line...

4. a tail...

5. a head...

6. a curved line... two ears... a muzzle... two lines like these...

7. eyes... nostrils... legs...

8. a mane... another leg... and hooves.

Your turn...

↘

How to draw a stable

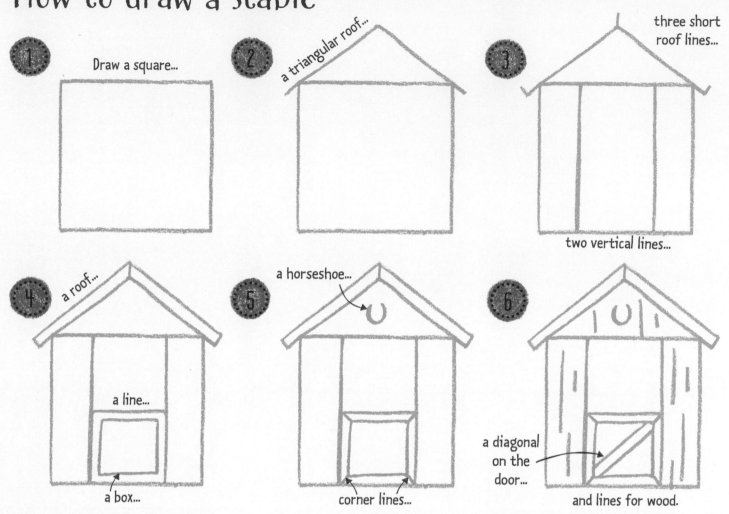

1 Draw a square...

2 a triangular roof...

3 three short roof lines... two vertical lines...

4 a roof... a line... a box...

5 a horseshoe... corner lines...

6 a diagonal on the door... and lines for wood.

Your turn...

How to draw a rearing horse

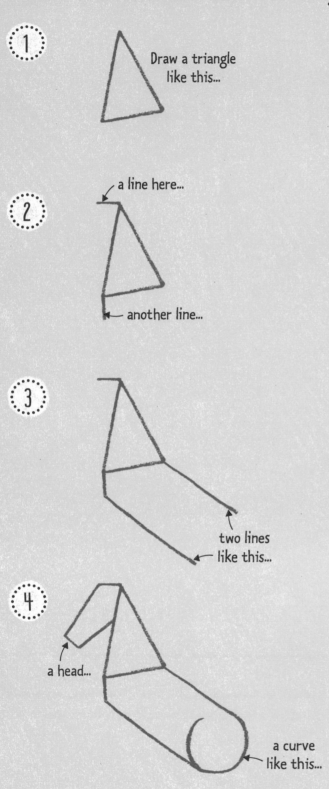

1 Draw a triangle like this...

2 a line here... / another line...

3 two lines like this...

4 a head... / a curve like this...

5 ears and a forelock... / a nose... / a curve... / triangular front legs... / and two back legs...

6 an eye... / a mane... / a tail... / four lower legs...

7 a nostril and mouth... / and fill in the forelock, mane and tail. / four hooves on each leg...

Your turn...

How to draw a Shire horse

Your turn...

1. Draw a square head and a triangular neck...

2. a rectangular body...

3. a tail... four legs...

4. ears and a forelock... an eye and a muzzle... furry legs...

5. a mane... a line... a nostril... and four hooves.

Shire horses are larger and bulkier than riding horses. They are also very strong.

How to draw a wagon

Your turn...

1 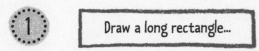 Draw a long rectangle...

2 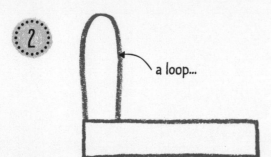 a loop...

3 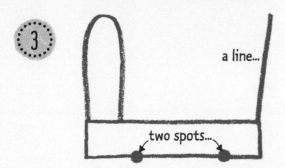 a line...

two spots...

4 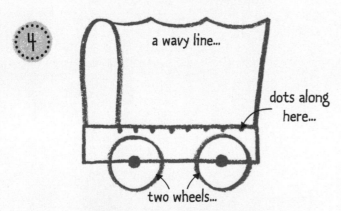 a wavy line...

dots along here...

two wheels...

5  two lines...

a curvy edge...

a shaft...

and spokes.

Try this...

You could copy this cart
and fill it with hay for a
horse to eat.

How to draw a fairground horse

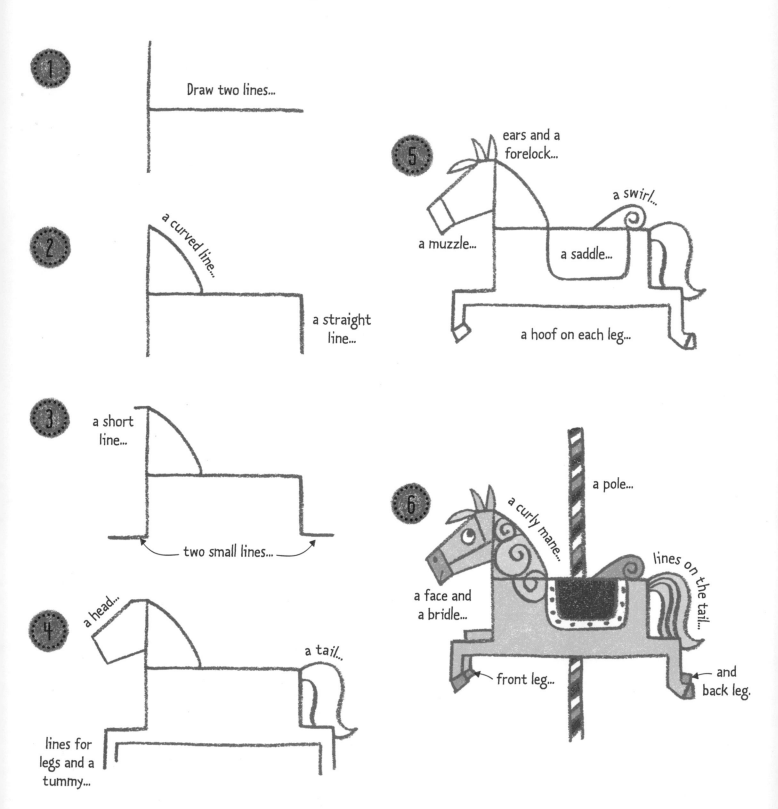

1 Draw two lines...

2 a curved line... a straight line...

3 a short line... two small lines...

4 a head... a tail... lines for legs and a tummy...

5 ears and a forelock... a swirl... a muzzle... a saddle... a hoof on each leg...

6 a pole... a curly mane... lines on the tail... a face and a bridle... front leg... and back leg.

38

Your turn...

How to draw a knight's horse

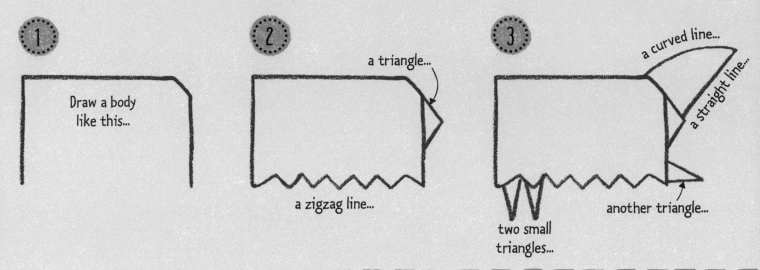

1 Draw a body like this...

2 a triangle... a zigzag line...

3 a curved line... a straight line... another triangle... two small triangles...

Your turn...

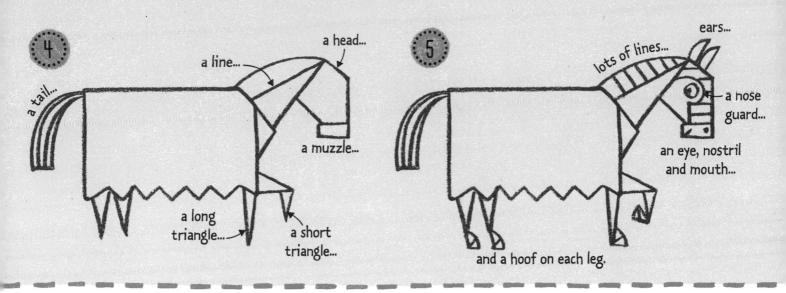

4 a tail... a line... a head...

a muzzle...

a long triangle...

a short triangle...

5 lots of lines... ears...

a hose guard...

an eye, nostril and mouth...

and a hoof on each leg.

Turn to the next page to find out how to draw a knight.

How to draw a knight

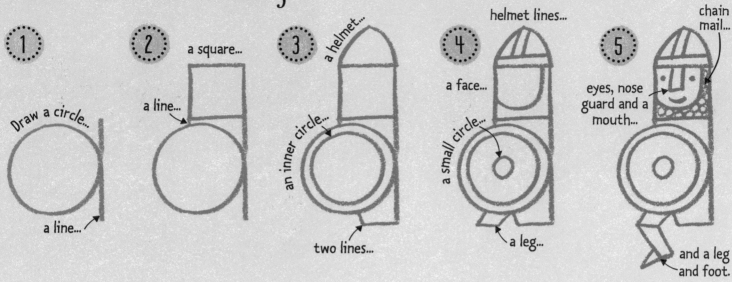

1 Draw a circle... a line...

2 a square... a line...

3 a helmet... an inner circle... two lines...

4 helmet lines... a face... a small circle... a leg...

5 chain mail... eyes, nose guard and a mouth... and a leg and foot.

Your turn...

42

Draw knights riding
on these horses.

43

How to draw a castle

1 Draw a rectangle... a door...

2 two tall rectangles...

3 towers...

4 triangular roofs... a line...

5 roof tiles... flags... door handles... and windows.

Your turn...

Try this...

Create a picture with
castles and knights riding
on horses (see pages 40–41
and 42–43).

How to draw a royal carriage

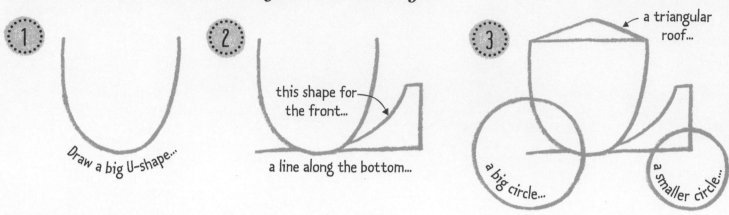

1 Draw a big U-shape...

2 this shape for the front...
a line along the bottom...

3 a triangular roof...
a big circle...
a smaller circle...

Your turn...

Add two lines like this to attach your carriages to a horse.

4

a crown...

windows...

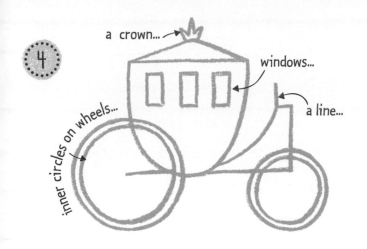

inner circles on wheels...

a line...

5

a seat...

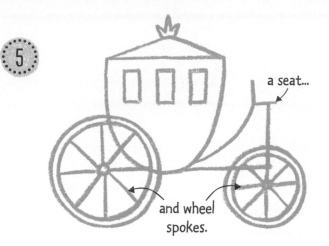

and wheel spokes.

How to draw a resting unicorn

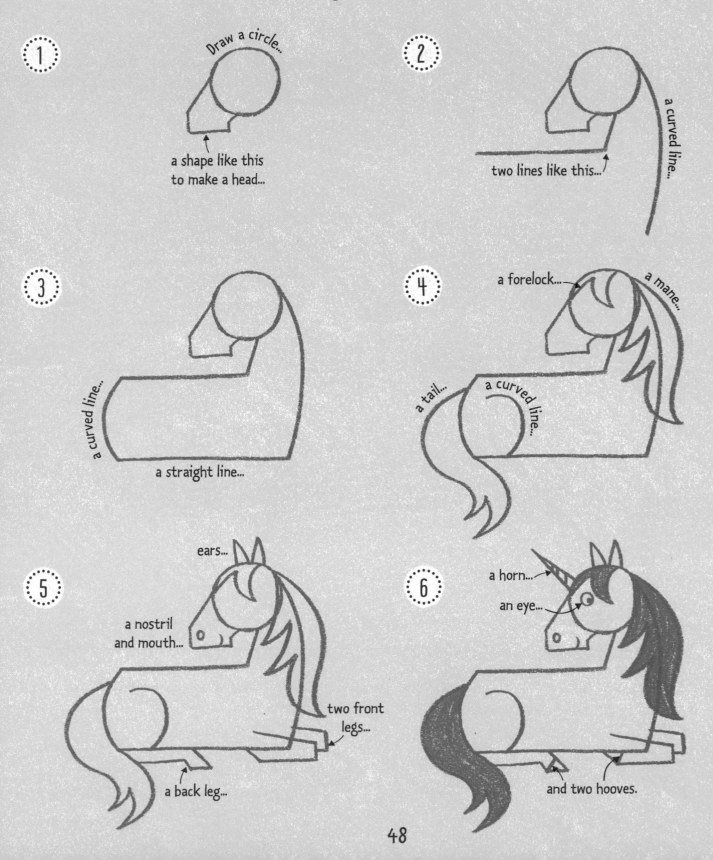

1. Draw a circle...

a shape like this to make a head...

2. a curved line...

two lines like this...

3. a curved line...

a straight line...

4. a forelock... a mane...

a tail...

a curved line...

5. ears...

a nostril and mouth...

two front legs...

a back leg...

6. a horn...

an eye...

and two hooves.

48

Your turn...

How to draw a leaping unicorn

1 Draw a circle...

2 a diamond... leave a small gap...

3 a diagonal line... a straight line... two lines... a curved line...

4 two ears... a nose... a front leg... a back leg...

Your turn...

5 a forelock...

a mane...

a tail...

another
back leg...

another
front leg...

6 a horn...

a face...

and hooves.

Try this...

Draw a rainbow and
add some stars.

How to draw a foal

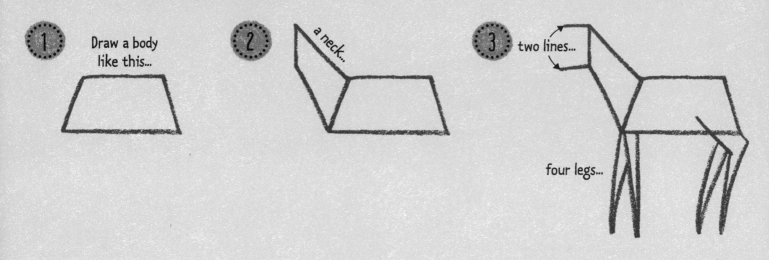

1 Draw a body like this...

2 a neck...

3 two lines...

four legs...

Your turn...

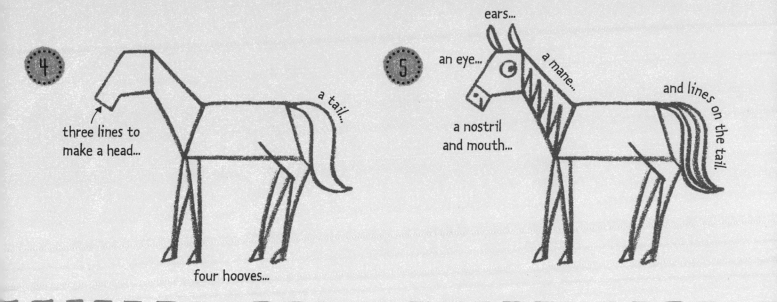

4 three lines to make a head...

a tail...

four hooves...

5 ears...

an eye...

a mane...

a nostril and mouth...

and lines on the tail.

How to draw a jumping horse

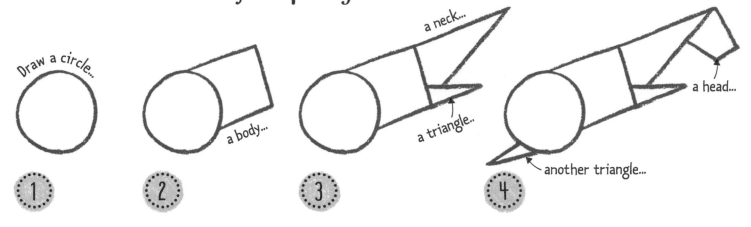

Draw a circle...

1

a body...

2

a neck...

a triangle..

3

a neck...

a head...

another triangle...

4

Your turn...

Try this...

Draw a simple fence for a horse to jump over.

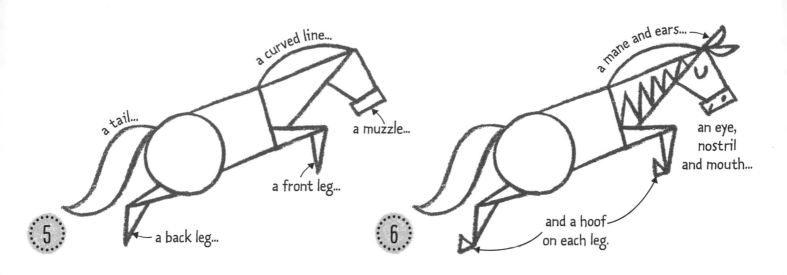

5

a tail...

a curved line...

a muzzle...

a front leg...

a back leg...

6

a mane and ears...

an eye, nostril and mouth...

and a hoof on each leg.

How to draw a fence...

1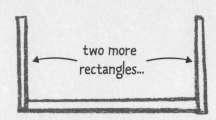
Draw a narrow rectangle...

2
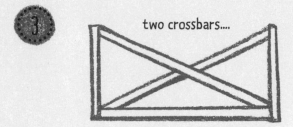
two more
rectangles...

3
two crossbars....
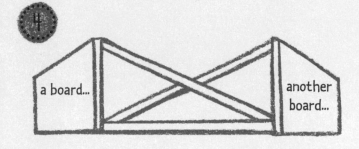

4
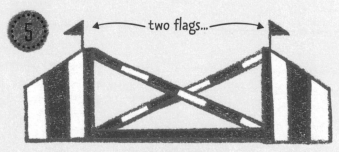
a board...
another
board...

5
two flags...
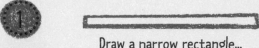
and add stripes.

...and another one

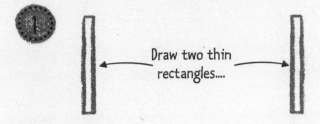

Draw two thin rectangles....

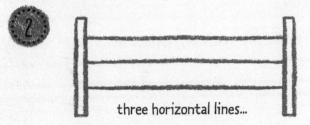

three horizontal lines...

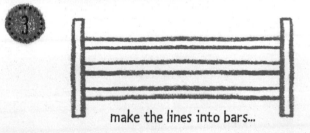

make the lines into bars...

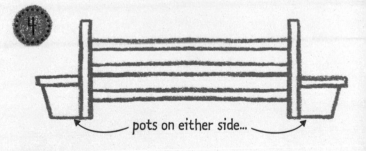

pots on either side...

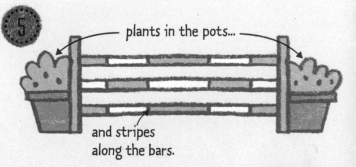

plants in the pots...

and stripes along the bars.

How to draw a rider

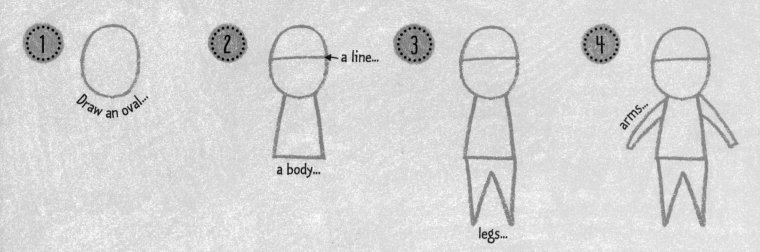

1 Draw an oval...

2 a line... a body...

3 legs...

4 arms...

Your turn...

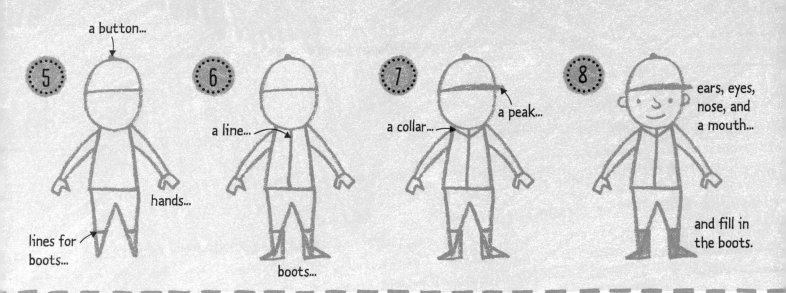

5. a button... hands... lines for boots...

6. a line... boots...

7. a collar... a peak...

8. ears, eyes, nose, and a mouth... and fill in the boots.

How to draw a horseshoe

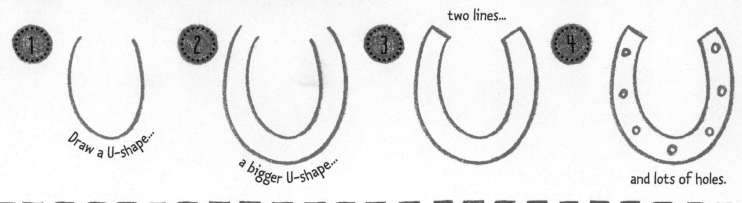

1 Draw a U-shape...

2 a bigger U-shape...

3 two lines...

4 and lots of holes.

Your turn...

Add horseshoes above the stable doors.

A halter

...and a bow

1  Draw a circle...

2 a triangular shape on each side...

3  four small lines...

4  and some ribbons.

Add a halter and a bow to this horse.

Draw a mane decorated with bows.

How to draw a dressage horse

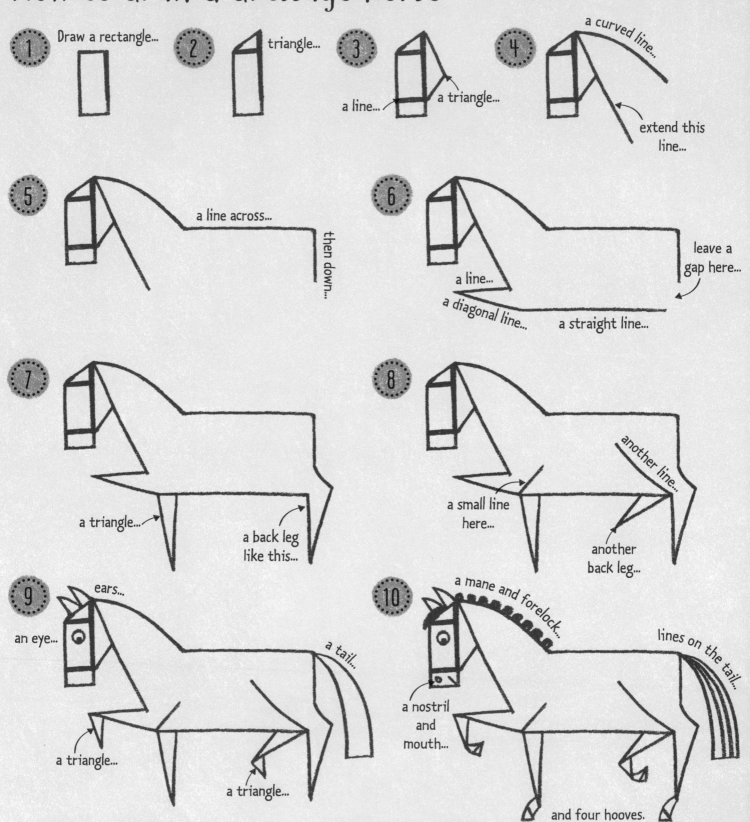

1 Draw a rectangle...

2 triangle...

3 a line... a triangle...

4 a curved line... extend this line...

5 a line across... then down...

6 a line... a diagonal line... a straight line... leave a gap here...

7 a triangle... a back leg like this...

8 another line... a small line here... another back leg...

9 ears... an eye... a triangle... a tail... a triangle...

10 a mane and forelock... lines on the tail... a nostril and mouth... and four hooves.

Your turn...

Dressage is a form of riding
where the horse performs precise
movements in response to signals
from the rider.

How to draw a dressage rider

1 Draw this shape...

2 a hat rim...

3 a triangular body...

4 an arm... the top of a leg...

5 a face... a hand... jacket tails... the lower leg...

6 a collar... an ear and hair... a foot... a saddle...

7 reins... and a stirrup.

Your turn...

Try this...

Add a rider to each trotting horse.

How to draw a horsebox

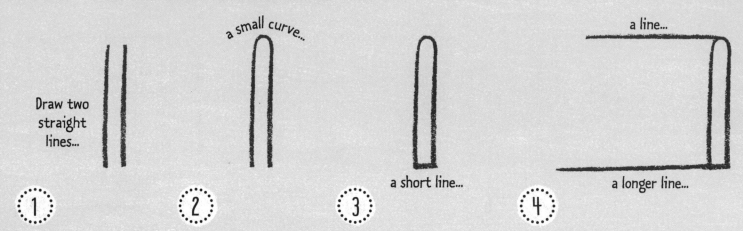

Draw two straight lines...

a small curve...

a short line...

a line...

a longer line...

1

2

3

4

Your turn...

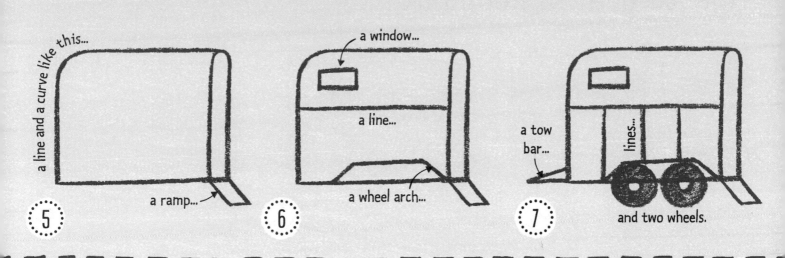

a line and a curve like this...

a ramp...

5

a window...

a line...

a wheel arch...

6

a tow bar...

lines...

and two wheels.

7

How to draw a Shetland pony

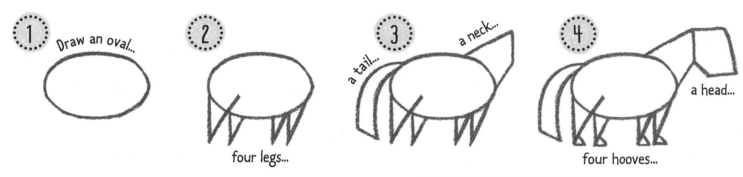

1 Draw an oval...

2 four legs...

3 a tail... a neck...

4 four hooves... a head...

Your turn...

Shetland ponies are a
breed of pony originally
from the Shetland Islands
of Scotland. They are small,
but strong, and have
thick shaggy manes.

5 lines on the tail... ears and a forelock... a nose...

6 a mane... lines on the forelock... and an eye, nose and mouth.

How to draw a pony rug

Your turn...

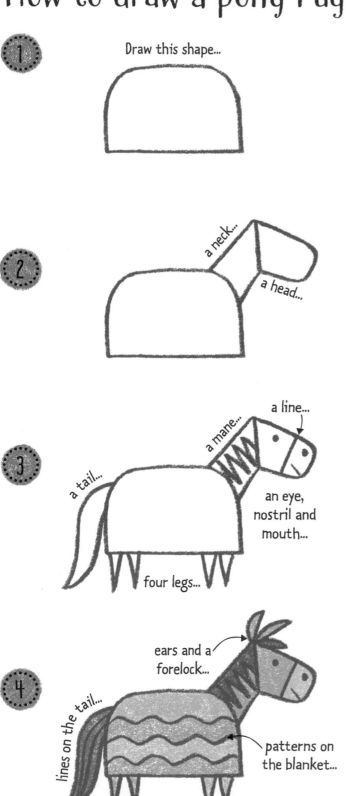

1 Draw this shape...

2 a neck...
a head...

3 a line...
a mane...
a tail...
an eye, nostril and mouth...
four legs...

4 ears and a forelock...
lines on the tail...
patterns on the blanket...
and hooves.

70

How to draw a donkey

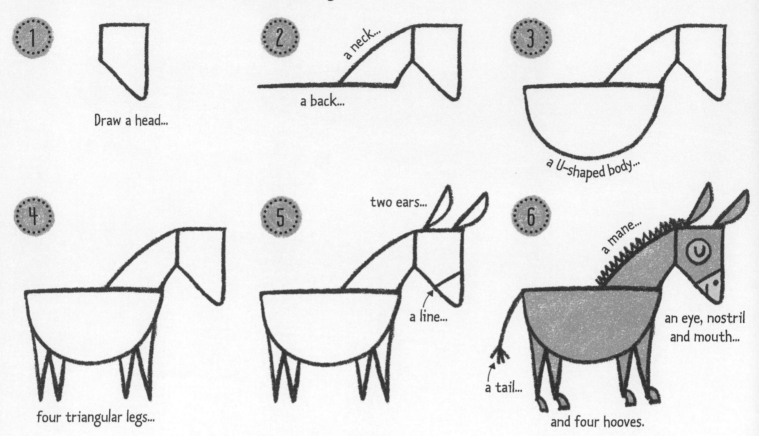

1 Draw a head...

2 a neck... a back...

3 a U-shaped body...

4 four triangular legs...

5 two ears... a line...

6 a mane... an eye, nostril and mouth... a tail... and four hooves.

Your turn...

Donkeys are not horses, but
come from the same family of
animals. They have thicker coats,
a shorter tail and longer ears.

In the fields

Add two more stables.

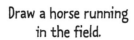

Draw a horse running
in the field.

Add more tufts
of grass.

74

Draw more trees in the distance.

Add more apples to the trees.

Draw another Shetland pony.

Draw more hay for the horses to eat.

Add a horse eating the hay.

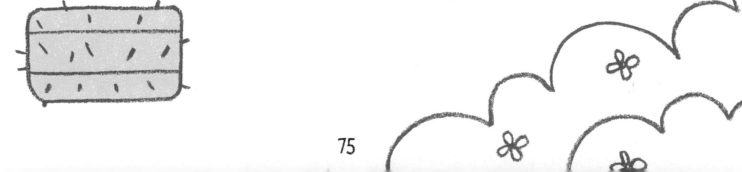

Horse show

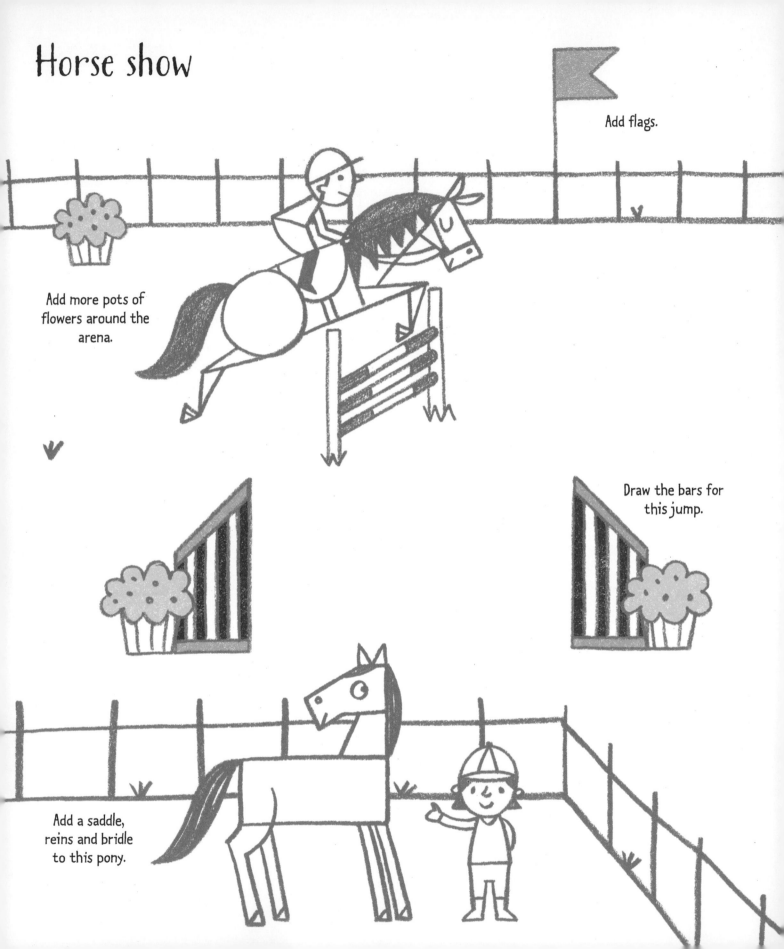

Add flags.

Add more pots of flowers around the arena.

Draw the bars for this jump.

Add a saddle, reins and bridle to this pony.

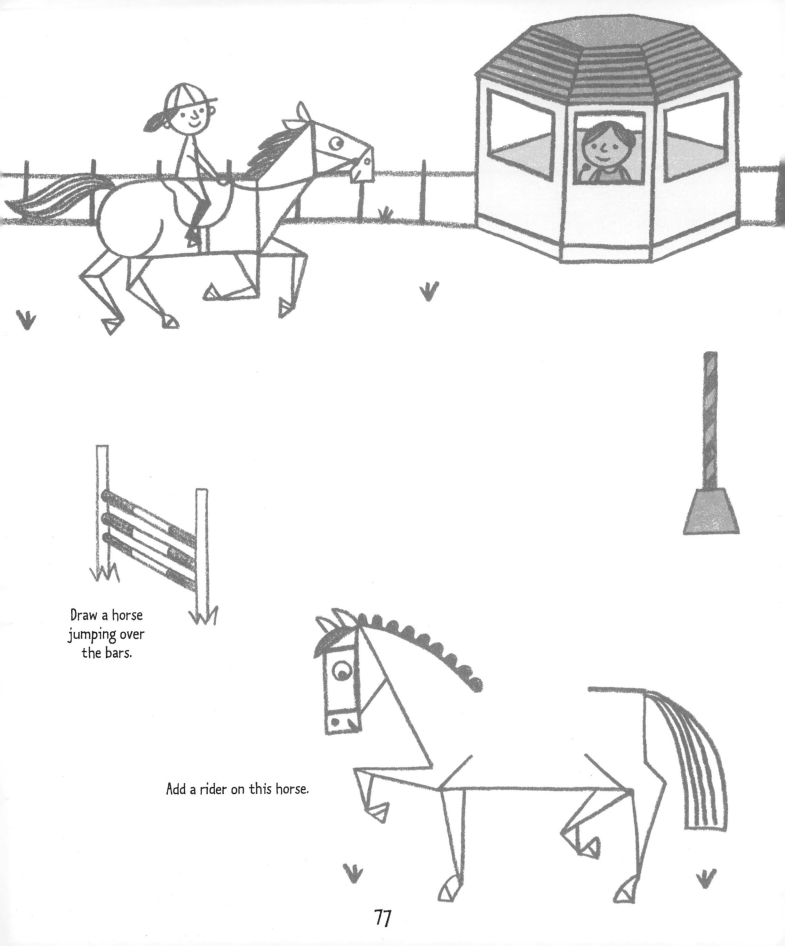

Draw a horse jumping over the bars.

Add a rider on this horse.

At the stables

Add more horses peering out of their stables.

• BLOSSOM •

Write names on the stable doors.

Draw more carrots.

Add someone leading this horse.

Add more hay.

Draw a saddle on its back.

Decorate this pony's blanket.

Draw a bucket of water for the thirsty ponies.

Draw an apple in this rider's hand.

Add a Shetland pony.

The winners

Draw more flags on the string.

Give each horse a ribbon.

Add some confetti in the air.

Draw a trophy in the winning rider's hand.

Draw two more riders on the podium.

Write 1st, 2nd and 3rd in the circles.

First published in 2020 by Usborne Publishing Limited, 83-85 Saffron Hill, London EC1N 8RT, United Kingdom. usborne.com